ART

ART

Biblical

TRUTHS

— for —

Creatives

B&H
PUBLISHING GROUP
NASHVILLE, TENNESSEE

978-1-5359-1784-1

Published by B&H Publishing Group
Nashville, Tennessee

Dewey Decimal Classification: 242.5
Subject Heading: DEVOTIONAL LITERATURE \
BIBLE—INSPIRATION \ MEDITATIONS \ PRAYERS

1 2 3 4 5 6 7 8 • 22 21 20 19 18

CONTENTS

CONTENTS

INTRODUCTION

If a person were to get online and type the word "art," they would be inundated with millions of images that would impress, confuse, anger, annoy, entrance, amaze, discomfort, amuse, bewilder, befuddle, and many others that would all have the same commonality. They would touch the soul in one form or another. Art connects. It's as simple as that. Whether we like it or not, art gives us something and we respond to it.

Some art can make the eyes water, while others will make them roll. Some art can soften a heart. Some can provide wisdom. Art is something that gets a reaction, whether the viewer, hearer, or reader likes it or not. That is a powerful thing. It is through inspiration and the gifts that God gives man, that man does something extraordinary . . . he creates.

In the world of psychology, there is a technique called art therapy. It encourages self-expression through painting, drawing, and sculpting. This allows for diagnosis, but also, psychologists have found that this style of therapy calms nervousness in those that go through this form of therapy. Allowing people to create in their own way is something that's good for the soul. Essentially, allowing people to use their God-given talents can soothe an anxious heart.

"Therefore I tell you: Don't worry about your life, what you will eat or what you will drink; or about your body, what you will wear. Isn't life more than food and the body more than clothing? Consider the birds of the sky: They don't sow or reap or gather into barns, yet your heavenly Father feeds them. Aren't you worth more than they? Can any of you add one moment to his life-span by worrying?"

   Matthew 6:25–27

———

Humble yourselves, therefore, under the mighty hand of God, so that he may exalt you at the proper time, casting all your cares on him, because he cares about you.

   1 Peter 5:6–7

"Peace I leave with you. My peace I give to you. I do not give to you as the world gives. Don't let your heart be troubled or fearful."

  John 14:27

———

Don't worry about anything, but in everything, through prayer and petition with thanksgiving, present your requests to God. And the peace of God, which surpasses all understanding, will guard your hearts and minds in Christ Jesus.

  Philippians 4:6–7

———

For God has not given us a spirit of fear, but one of power, love, and sound judgment.

  2 Timothy 1:7

Heavenly Father, I am nervous. There are things going on in my life that I feel are outside of my control. Father, I know that, with You, there is nothing that I cannot handle. Be with me, Lord, as I walk through this time. Take away my anxious spirit, and replace it with Your peace. Amen

Claude Monet is known as one of the great impressionists in the art world. The impressionists were known for capturing the beauty found in the simplicity of the surrounding world. His painting, *Poppies in a Field,* captures that very idea of beauty in simplicity. If you ever see the painting, you'll notice that there are people in the painting, but the overall beauty of God's scenery is so overwhelming that it's easy to overlook them.

I have asked one thing from the LORD*;*
it is what I desire:
to dwell in the house of the LORD
all the days of my life,
gazing on the beauty of the LORD
and seeking him in his temple.

    Psalm 27:4

———

I will praise you
because I have been remarkably and wondrously
made.
Your works are wondrous,
and I know this very well.

    Psalm 139:14

Charm is deceptive and beauty is fleeting,
but a woman who fears the LORD *will be praised.*
    Proverbs 31:30

———

You are absolutely beautiful, my darling;
there is no imperfection in you.
    Song of Songs 4:7

———

Don't let your beauty consist of outward things like
elaborate hairstyles and wearing gold jewelry, but
rather what is inside the heart—the imperishable
quality of a gentle and quiet spirit, which is of great
worth in God's sight.
    1 Peter 3:3–4

Lord, there is so much in this world that You have created that is so beautiful. Thank You, Father, for making a world that is filled with such beauty. Lord, allow me to continue to notice the beautiful moments that You have created in my life. Allow me to respond to these moments with thankfulness and awe. Amen

There's an artist named Matthew Allen that has a print called *Count Your Blessings*. It's a simple piece. It is merely a page filled from top to bottom with tallies, and at the top of the page are the words "Count Your Blessings." It is a simple message with a great deal of weight. How many of us take the time to actually count our blessings? When we think of all the little things that God has blessed us with, we find that our list of tallies can become just as innumerable.

"May the LORD bless you and protect you; may the LORD make his face shine on you and be gracious to you; may the LORD look with favor on you and give you peace."

Numbers 6:24–26

———

Indeed, we have all received grace upon grace from his fullness, for the law was given through Moses; grace and truth came through Jesus Christ.

John 1:16–17

———

And God is able to make every grace overflow to you, so that in every way, always having everything you need, you may excel in every good work.

2 Corinthians 9:8

Blessed is the God and Father of our Lord Jesus Christ, who has blessed us with every spiritual blessing in the heavens in Christ.

Ephesians 1:3

———

And my God will supply all your needs according to his riches in glory in Christ Jesus.

Philippians 4:19

Lord God, I know that there are so many things in this life that You have provided that I take for granted. I know that there are so many blessings that You have given me that go unnoticed. Father, instill in me a thankful spirit that takes note of all of the little things that You provide in my life. Allow me to look at my surroundings and not see them as expectations, but blessings. Amen

One of the boldest moves in the art world was the move to Impressionism. There are entire classes taught on this, so to put it short, artists would paint their surroundings and capture exactly what was shown. This was called realism. Impressionists, however, would focus on capturing the colors with broad strokes to give the viewer an *impression* of what was being shown. Many artists that moved to this style were shunned, but their art has come to be some of the most appreciated pieces in cultural history. Like impressionists, God calls us to live a life that is bold and different from the surrounding world.

The wicked flee when no one is pursuing them,
but the righteous are as bold as a lion.
  Proverbs 28:1

———

Since, then, we have such a hope, we act with great
boldness.
  2 Corinthians 3:12

———

In him we have boldness and confident access
through faith in him.
  Ephesians 3:12

For God has not given us a spirit of fear, but one of power, love, and sound judgment.

    2 Timothy 1:7

———

Therefore, let us approach the throne of grace with boldness, so that we may receive mercy and find grace to help us in time of need.

    Hebrews 4:16

Lord, I so often walk through this world only wanting to blend in. Father, I know that is not right. I know that I am called to walk differently. Lord God, instill in me a spirit of boldness to walk in the way in which You would have me go. Amen

There was an elderly woman preparing for death. Doctors had told her that her systems were failing and that it was only a matter of time. Seeking comfort, she spent her last days seeing family and listening to some of her records. She spent each day listening to a different time period. She started with choirs, then recorded hymns, then finally listened to praise and worship bands on the radio. When asked why she listened to all of the different kinds of music, she said, "It brings me comfort to know that no matter how much the music has changed, God has stayed constant."

Even when I go through the darkest valley,
I fear no danger,
for you are with me;
your rod and your staff—they comfort me.
   Psalm 23:4

———

Remember your word to your servant;
you have given me hope through it.
This is my comfort in my affliction:
Your promise has given me life.
   Psalm 119:49–50

———

As a mother comforts her son, so I will comfort you,
and you will be comforted in Jerusalem.
   Isaiah 66:13

"Blessed are those who mourn, for they will be comforted."

Matthew 5:4

———

Blessed be the God and Father of our Lord Jesus Christ, the Father of mercies and the God of all comfort. He comforts us in all our affliction, so that we may be able to comfort those who are in any kind of affliction, through the comfort we ourselves receive from God.

2 Corinthians 1:3–4

Heavenly Father, thank You for giving me comfort in the uncomfortable times. Thank You for being there when no one else was. Lord, right now I am crushed, I need Your comfort, God. Allow me to lay down my pride and seek comfort from You, Lord. Amen

One of the things that any writer, musician, or artist will tell you is that there is a need to be confident in their world. In order to sell a book, song, or piece of art, a person needs to know how to sell themselves. That can only be done with confidence. This kind of confidence has also let these people down from time to time. Something we can know confidently is that God never fails. Regardless of the confidence we try to build up for ourselves . . . we can have confidence in knowing that God always is, and always will be.

Do not fear, for I am with you; do not be afraid, for I am your God. I will strengthen you; I will help you; I will hold on to you with my righteous right hand.

  Isaiah 41:10

―――

It is not that we are competent in ourselves to claim anything as coming from ourselves, but our adequacy is from God.

  2 Corinthians 3:5

―――

I am able to do all things through him who strengthens me.

  Philippians 4:13

So don't throw away your confidence, which has a great reward. For you need endurance, so that after you have done God's will, you may receive what was promised.

Hebrews 10:35–36

———

This is how we will know that we belong to the truth and will reassure our hearts before him whenever our hearts condemn us; for God is greater than our hearts, and he knows all things. Dear friends, if our hearts don't condemn us, we have confidence before God and receive whatever we ask from him because we keep his commands and do what is pleasing in his sight.

1 John 3:19–22

Father, right now I feel so insecure. I feel that there is nothing I can do to succeed. I know that I'm holding myself back because of my lack of confidence. Father, give me the confidence to take on all of the things before me. Allow me to know that is through You that I can do all things. Father, allow me to move forward with You so that I can walk confidently. Amen

Creativity is the common thread between all types of artists. It is a gift that has many different styles but still comes from that same source of a creative spirit. Most of us have a creative part of our brains. Some of us choose to use it more than others, but the fact is that it is a gift. This gift from God is what is used to bring goodness into the world. Some use their creativity for terrible reasons; others choose to glorify God. God gives us all gifts, but it is up to us to decide whether we will use them to corrupt others even more or to bring glory to God.

So God created man in his own image; he created him in the image of God; he created them male and female.

    Genesis 1:27

———

All things were created through him, and apart from him not one thing was created that has been created.

    John 1:3

———

Do you see a person skilled in his work?
He will stand in the presence of kings.
He will not stand in the presence of the unknown.

    Proverbs 22:29

I will praise you
because I have been remarkably and wondrously
made.
Your works are wondrous,
and I know this very well.
    Psalm 139:14

———

For we are his workmanship, created in Christ Jesus
for good works, which God prepared ahead of time
for us to do.
    Ephesians 2:10

Lord, thank You for giving us the ability to be creative. Like most gifts, I know that this one comes with a purpose. Father, remind me that the creativity You have given me comes with the purpose to glorify You. Amen

Just about every kindergarten class in the world makes the terrible mistake of having a day for the children to finger-paint. Some of you as parents have decided to do this in your own home. Paint splotches seem to go on places other than the paper or canvas. It's a mess. So why do we do it? It's because there is a joy and delight that we see on a child's face when they get to create. Even though it's messy, we prepare kids to be able to learn the importance of creating something, and we can't say no to the kind of delight a child has when they create something they're proud of.

How happy is the one who does not
walk in the advice of the wicked
or stand in the pathway with sinners
or sit in the company of mockers!
Instead, his delight is in the LORD's instruction,
and he meditates on it day and night.
He is like a tree planted beside flowing streams
that bears its fruit in its season
and whose leaf does not wither.
Whatever he does prospers.

    Psalm 1:1–3

———

He brought me out to a spacious place;
he rescued me because he delighted in me.

    Psalm 18:19

Take delight in the LORD,
and he will give you your heart's desires.
   Psalm 37:4

———

If your instruction had not been my delight,
I would have died in my affliction.
I will never forget your precepts,
for you have given me life through them.
   Psalm 119:92–93

———

"The LORD your God is among you, a warrior who
saves. He will rejoice over you with gladness. He
will be quiet in his love. He will delight in you with
singing."
   Zephaniah 3:17

Heavenly Father, thank You for all of the moments that I take delight in. Father, continue to give those moments. Allow me to be able to take delight in the moments You have provided. Father, instill in me a spirit that strives to take delight in You. Amen

DISCERNMENT

There is a great deal of discernment that goes into art. Ask any artist and they will tell you they've all stared at a blank canvas at least once—debating on what direction they should go. There was an artist that once said the hardest part of art is deciding what story you want your image to tell. For him, that story depends on color, shading, form, expression, and countless other variables. This all happens before he even picks up a brush. God calls us to act similarly. Sometimes we are so impulsive that we are unwilling to think before we act.

So give your servant a receptive heart to judge your people and to discern between good and evil. For who is able to judge this great people of yours?

1 Kings 3:9

———

And I pray this: that your love will keep on growing in knowledge and every kind of discernment, so that you may approve the things that are superior and may be pure and blameless in the day of Christ.

Philippians 1:9–10

———

Don't stifle the Spirit. Don't despise prophecies, but test all things. Hold on to what is good. Stay away from every kind of evil.

1 Thessalonians 5:19–22

Now if any of you lacks wisdom, he should ask God—who gives to all generously and ungrudgingly—and it will be given to him.

James 1:5

———

Dear friends, do not believe every spirit, but test the spirits to see if they are from God, because many false prophets have gone out into the world.

1 John 4:1

Lord, because of my impatience, I have made decisions without thinking. I have acted without thoughtfulness. Father, forgive me for not acting wisely, and allow me to make decisions well in the future. Lord, give me the ability to move forward with discernment. Amen

Most authors, poets, and writers will normally struggle with satisfaction. Most have heard of the student that's never satisfied with their work. There was a student in a poetry class that would always take an extra day to turn in the work. The professor had finally had enough and asked why she would take so long. Her response was that the work was never perfect. The professor responded, "I didn't ask you to do perfection. I asked you to do your best." There are times we strive for perfection, but that's not how it works. Christ is what makes our lives satisfactory, not any acts of "perfection" we try to make for ourselves.

For he has satisfied the thirsty
and filled the hungry with good things.
   Psalm 107:9

———

You open your hand
and satisfy the desire of every living thing.
   Psalm 145:16

———

The LORD will always lead you,
satisfy you in a parched land,
and strengthen your bones.
You will be like a watered garden
and like a spring whose water never runs dry.
   Isaiah 58:11

"I am the bread of life," Jesus told them. "No one who comes to me will ever be hungry, and no one who believes in me will ever be thirsty again."

    John 6:35

———

Now may the God of hope fill you with all joy and peace as you believe so that you may overflow with hope by the power of the Holy Spirit.

    Romans 15:13

Father, I am sorry. I know that I have acted dissatisfied. I feel like nothing I do is enough. Lord, allow me to walk forward in life knowing that not every little thing has to be perfect. Father, put in me a spirit of acceptance that will have a focus on You. Thank You for always satisfying. Amen

One of the most famous statues in the world is found at the top of a mountain in Rio de Janeiro. Most of the world knows it as the "Jesus Statue," but its official designation is "Christ the Redeemer." The statue stands over the city with outstretched arms, as a symbol of peace, a symbol that has encouraged the world in knowing that Christ is over the world and waiting with outstretched arms for us to answer His call.

The LORD is the one who will go before you. He will be with you; he will not leave you or abandon you. Do not be afraid or discouraged.

  Deuteronomy 31:8

———

God is our refuge and strength,
a helper who is always found
in times of trouble.

  Psalm 46:1

———

"Aren't five sparrows sold for two pennies? Yet not one of them is forgotten in God's sight. Indeed, the hairs of your head are all counted. Don't be afraid; you are worth more than many sparrows."

  Luke 12:6–7

"*I have told you these things so that in me you may have peace. You will have suffering in this world. Be courageous! I have conquered the world.*"

John 16:33

———

And let us watch out for one another to provoke love and good works, not neglecting to gather together, as some are in the habit of doing, but encouraging each other, and all the more as you see the day approaching.

Hebrews 10:24–25

Lord God, there are so many moments in life when I am discouraged. I know that there are things that will come that will bring sorrow, but Father, be with me. Continue to encourage me each day. Thank You for giving me strength. Amen

In Indonesia, there are paintings on the walls of caves that date back 40,000 years. Art does stand the test of time; that is so true. Paintings, writings, and songs all outlive their creators, but nothing in this world will last forever. The cave paintings will fade . . . the Mona Lisa is already beginning to dull. The one thing that has always been and always will be is God and His love for us.

Before the mountains were born,
before you gave birth to the earth and the world,
from eternity to eternity, you are God.
　　Psalm 90:2

———

He has made everything appropriate in its time.
He has also put eternity in their hearts, but no one
can discover the work God has done from beginning
to end.
　　Ecclesiastes 3:11

———

"This is eternal life: that they may know you, the
only true God, and the one you have sent—Jesus
Christ."
　　John 17:3

"Truly I tell you, anyone who hears my word and believes him who sent me has eternal life and will not come under judgment but has passed from death to life."

John 5:24

———

For the wages of sin is death, but the gift of God is eternal life in Christ Jesus our Lord.

Romans 6:23

Heavenly Father, thank You for giving me a love that will last forever. Father, there are so many things that I hold onto in this world, but I know that it is You that I should hold onto. Father, in all things that I do, please allow me to remember that the things of this world are temporary, but it is You and Your love that is eternal. Amen

F. Scott Fitzgerald was the author of one of the most famous works of literature in modern American history. Though *The Great Gatsby* is read in high schools all over the country, publishers would often tell Fitzgerald that he would have quite an amazing story if he simply got rid of "that Gatsby character." Anyone who's read the book can tell you how silly a statement like that is. Nevertheless, Fitzgerald had to deal with failure. Did he simply put the manuscript on the shelf? No! He moved forward. Do we allow failure to keep us from moving forward? Do we allow failure to disable us, or do we have faith?

He brought me up from a desolate pit, out of the muddy clay, and set my feet on a rock, making my steps secure. He put a new song in my mouth, a hymn of praise to our God. Many will see and fear, and they will trust in the LORD.

    Psalm 40:2–3

———

Now we have this treasure in clay jars, so that this extraordinary power may be from God and not from us. We are afflicted in every way but not crushed; we are perplexed but not in despair; we are persecuted but not abandoned; we are struck down but not destroyed.

    2 Corinthians 4:7–9

A person's steps are established by the Lord,
and he takes pleasure in his way.
Though he falls, he will not be overwhelmed,
because the Lord *supports him with his hand.*
Psalm 37:23–24

———

And not only that, but we also rejoice in our
afflictions, because we know that affliction
produces endurance, endurance produces proven
character, and proven character produces hope.
Romans 5:3–4

Lord Jesus, I have failed. I put effort into something and that effort didn't pay off the way I wanted it to. Lord, please remind me that a failure is only permanent if I allow it to be. Work in my heart and encourage me to know that it is through You that I can do all things. Lord Jesus, allow me to move past this failure and take forward facing steps again. Amen

There's something about presenting your work to others. It's a terrible emotion. Some artists have said that it can make a person love their art more or hate it altogether. It's amazing how we can let fear take control of us like that; how we can look at our own creations and love them or hate them because of our desire for approval and fear of rejection. Fear is something that can only affect you if you allow it, and we are a people called to move above that fear and live courageously.

Haven't I commanded you: be strong and courageous? Do not be afraid or discouraged, for the LORD your God is with you wherever you go.
  Joshua 1:9

———

*When I am afraid,
I will trust in you.*
  Psalm 56:3

———

You did not receive a spirit of slavery to fall back into fear. Instead, you received the Spirit of adoption, by whom we cry out, "Abba, Father!"
  Romans 8:15

For God has not given us a spirit of fear, but one of power, love, and sound judgment.

2 Timothy 1:7

———

Humble yourselves, therefore, under the mighty hand of God, so that he may exalt you at the proper time, casting all your cares on him, because he cares about you.

1 Peter 5:6–7

Father, I have allowed fear to keep me from accomplishing great things. I have allowed it to fester in me, and I cannot do anything without the fear of failure. Lord, work in me to be able to overcome these fears. I know that if I am with You, then I have nothing to fear. Continue to stay with me, Lord. Allow me to never forget that You are always with me. Amen

Something you'll sometimes see in a coffee shop is a group of writers huddled together—saying nothing and typing diligently. If you keep moving, you'll miss something special. One of the writers will lift his or her head from the screen and ask a question of the others. They want feedback. The others will perk up, listen intently, and share their thoughts. This person is seeking sharpening, comradery, honesty, and opportunity from the other writers. This group chooses each other to grow deeper relationships; and out of those relationships, they become better at their craft. Are we surrounding ourselves with people that make us better? Are we sharpening and being sharpened?

Iron sharpens iron,
and one person sharpens another.
    Proverbs 27:17

———

Two are better than one because they have a good
reward for their efforts. For if either falls, his
companion can lift him up; but pity the one who
falls without another to lift him up.
    Ecclesiastes 4:9–10

———

Carry one another's burdens; in this way you will
fulfill the law of Christ.
    Galatians 6:2

*Therefore encourage one another and build each
other up as you are already doing.*

   1 Thessalonians 5:11

———

*And let us watch out for one another to provoke love
and good works, not neglecting to gather together,
as some are in the habit of doing, but encouraging
each other, and all the more as you see the day
approaching.*

   Hebrews 10:24–25

Lord, thank You for the people in my life that make me better. They are more than friends; they are people that make me better in all aspects of life. Father, thank You for the fellowship in my life; allow these people to continue to stay in my life. Allow them to continue to sharpen me, and allow me to sharpen them. Amen

Some of the most moving songs and stories in history have all centered around the concept of forgiveness. Some songs talk about heartbreak. Some discuss fights that went too far, and some simply say "I'm sorry" for an unmentioned wrong. Why do these stories move us? I believe it's because we all seek relationships so badly that when one is broken, there is a desire to mend. We have a natural pull toward reconciliation when there is a wedge between us and the ones we've wronged. Do we seek to remove the wedges between ourselves and those we've hurt? Do we seek to remove the wedge that keeps us from reconciliation with God?

"Therefore I tell you, her many sins have been forgiven; that's why she loved much. But the one who is forgiven little, loves little."
  Luke 7:47

———

Live in harmony with one another. Do not be proud; instead, associate with the humble. Do not be wise in your own estimation. Do not repay anyone evil for evil. Give careful thought to do what is honorable in everyone's eyes. If possible, as far as it depends on you, live at peace with everyone.
  Romans 12:16–18

*Be kind and compassionate to one another,
forgiving one another, just as God also forgave you
in Christ.*

   Ephesians 4:32

———

*As God's chosen ones, holy and dearly loved, put on
compassion, kindness, humility, gentleness, and
patience, bearing with one another and forgiving
one another if anyone has a grievance against
another. Just as the Lord has forgiven you, so you
are also to forgive.*

   Colossians 3:12–13

Heavenly Father, please soften my heart. There is someone who has hurt me. I don't want to forgive them, but I know I need to. If I hold onto this anger, I know it will only grow to bitterness. I know that it will keep me from loving this person. Father, please instill in me a spirit of forgiveness so that I may replace the anger I have for this person with love. Amen

One of the most famous friendships in the literary world belonged to C. S. Lewis and J. R. R. Tolkien. Many people familiar with the literary world would probably tell you that without this friendship, we might have never seen *The Lord of the Rings* or *The Chronicles of Narnia*. In today's time, people normally get so hung up on the concept of what friendship can do for themselves, but we never think about what a friendship can bring to others. Thank God for your friends; the relationship may be more impactful than you realize.

Iron sharpens iron,
and one person sharpens another.
  Proverbs 27:17

––––––

Two are better than one because they have a good
reward for their efforts. For if either falls, his
companion can lift him up; but pity the one who
falls without another to lift him up.
  Ecclesiastes 4:9–10

––––––

Dear friends, let us love one another, because love is
from God, and everyone who loves has been born of
God and knows God.
  1 John 4:7

"No one has greater love than this: to lay down his life for his friends. You are my friends if you do what I command you. I do not call you servants anymore, because a servant doesn't know what his master is doing. I have called you friends, because I have made known to you everything I have heard from my Father."

John 15:13–15

———

Therefore encourage one another and build each other up as you are already doing.

1 Thessalonians 5:11

Lord, thank You for friends. Allow me to always work to be a better one. Father, allow my friendships to be able to show You. Allow people to see that the common thread of the friendship is that there is a relationship with You. Lord, allow me to be a better friend to others. Thank You for being my friend . . . the best I could ever ask for. Amen

Happiness is such a difficult emotion. There are so many people that can feign happiness. All it takes is a smile and *Voila!* you're happy. We all know that's not necessarily true. One of the most famous smiles in art history is the Mona Lisa, not because we see her teeth, or catch her mid laugh, but because it's honest. The smile is a faint smirk, whatever happiness she has, is her own. It is something that has plagued the minds of most historians. Why does she smile? It is unknown, but we can't escape how real it feels. Happiness is something that can be faked, but God has called us to be honest in all things . . . even our smiles.

Therefore my heart is glad
and my whole being rejoices;
my body also rests securely.
    Psalm 16:9

––––––

Take delight in the LORD,
and he will give you your heart's desires.
    Psalm 37:4

––––––

A joyful heart makes a face cheerful,
but a sad heart produces a broken spirit.
    Proverbs 15:13

I know that there is nothing better for them than to rejoice and enjoy the good life.

Ecclesiastes 3:12

———

Rejoice in the Lord always. I will say it again: Rejoice!

Philippians 4:4

Father, thank You for the happy times. Thank You for the times in which I am genuinely happy. Father, allow me to be genuine with my happiness. Allow me to spread that happiness to others. Lord, allow others to know that my reason for happiness stems from my relationship with You. Amen

Somewhere Over the Rainbow is a simple song with a simple message: hope. There is a place where things seem to be perfect. It's just over the rainbow. There's something to that idea . . . a place worth being just on the other side of a rainbow. It's a place man cannot get to on his own, but it's there. A lot like the Father, there is only one way to Him. It's impossible for us to make it there on our own. For that, we need Christ.

But those who trust in the LORD
will renew their strength;
they will soar on wings like eagles;
they will run and not become weary,
they will walk and not faint.

    Isaiah 40:31

———

We have also obtained access through him by faith
into this grace in which we stand, and we rejoice in
the hope of the glory of God. And not only that, but
we also rejoice in our afflictions, because we know
that affliction produces endurance, endurance
produces proven character, and proven character
produces hope.

    Romans 5:2–4

*I wait for the LORD; I wait
and put my hope in his word.*
    Psalm 130:5

———

*Now may the God of hope fill you with all joy and
peace as you believe so that you may overflow with
hope by the power of the Holy Spirit.*
    Romans 15:13

Lord Jesus, thank You for being the hope of mankind. Thank You for dying on the cross so that I may be with You forever. Lord, there are moments that I forget about the hope in my l ife. I get discouraged so easily because I take my eyes off You, Lord. Be with me, Jesus; continue giving me hope each day. Amen

HUMILITY

If someone mentions Mr. Rogers, most know exactly who they're talking about. Mr. Rogers was known for teaching children the importance of respect, learning, and a love for the arts, but he was also a walking example of humility. It was because of his famous humility that once when his car was stolen, the local radio published the news and the car was returned with an apology note attached to it. Though we rarely see humility today, it is always something that is respected when it is seen.

Sitting down, he called the Twelve and said to them, "If anyone wants to be first, he must be last and servant of all."

    Mark 9:35

————

Live in harmony with one another. Do not be proud; instead, associate with the humble. Do not be wise in your own estimation.

    Romans 12:16

————

Do nothing out of selfish ambition or conceit, but in humility consider others as more important than yourselves.

    Philippians 2:3

*Adopt the same attitude as that of Christ Jesus,
who, existing in the form of God, did not consider
equality with God as something to be exploited.
Instead he emptied himself by assuming the form
of a servant, taking on the likeness of humanity.
And when he had come as a man, he humbled
himself by becoming obedient to the point of
death—even to death on a cross.*

    Philippians 2:5–8

———

*Who among you is wise and understanding? By
his good conduct he should show that his works are
done in the gentleness that comes from wisdom.*

    James 3:13

Father, remind me daily to lay down my pride. I have acted in ways that have not shown humility. I have allowed my actions and attitude to show a proud spirit. Lord, put in me a spirit of humility so that I may better serve others . . . so that I may better serve You. Amen

JOY

Dr. Seuss once wrote, "Don't cry because it's over. Smile because it happened." There's wisdom in that. In life, we have this tendency to become depressed when the good times end. We believe the bad must begin. When the weekend is over, you're doomed to go to work. When loved ones leave us, we have to be alone. The reality is that joy is determined by our perspective. A funeral is not a time to mourn so much as it is an opportunity to celebrate life. A moving away is not so much a leaving as much as it is moving to another adventure. Joy is something that is more than just simple happiness; it is an attitude of excitement for what is to come.

You reveal the path of life to me;
in your presence is abundant joy;
at your right hand are eternal pleasures.

Psalm 16:11

———

*This is the day the L*ORD *has made;*
let us rejoice and be glad in it.

Psalm 118:24

But the fruit of the Spirit is love, joy, peace,
patience, kindness, goodness, faithfulness,
gentleness, and self-control. The law is not against
such things.

 Galatians 5:22–23

———

As the Father has loved me, I have also loved you.
Remain in my love. If you keep my commands
you will remain in my love, just as I have kept my
Father's commands and remain in his love. I have
told you these things so that my joy may be in you
and your joy may be complete.

 John 15:9–11

Heavenly Father, I have allowed myself to lose my joy. I have allowed the things in life that bring me down to keep me down. Father, allow me to respond to the negative with joy. Put in me a joyful heart that looks at the negative as an opportunity for the good. Amen

Sometimes we hear stories about the painstaking work of some artists. One that is often brought to our knowledge is Michelangelo. His work in the Sistine Chapel is often cited as one of the greatest feats ever completed in art history. It took him four years, and he had to build scaffolding that would allow him to lie on his back for prolonged amounts of time in order to finish it. The fact is that the best things in life require the greatest of efforts. Laziness is never an acceptable quality in the process of achieving greatness.

The slacker craves, yet has nothing,
but the diligent is fully satisfied.
    Proverbs 13:4

—————

The one who is lazy in his work
is brother to a vandal.
    Proverbs 18:9

Whatever you do, do it from the heart, as something done for the Lord and not for people, knowing that you will receive the reward of an inheritance from the Lord. You serve the Lord Christ.

Colossians 3:23–24

———

In fact, when we were with you, this is what we commanded you: "If anyone isn't willing to work, he should not eat."

2 Thessalonians 3:10

Lord God, forgive me. I have taken on a lazy spirit. I have allowed rest to turn into laziness. I know that through You I can accomplish great things; but in order to accomplish anything I have to be willing to get up and move. Father, instill in me an attitude that is hardworking. You do not deserve a lazy spirit, Lord. Allow me to shake it and move to action. Amen

There is nothing quite like a good book dedication. Authors use this moment to point to those that inspired them to write the book in the first place. In *The Heart of a Goof,* P. G. WodeHouse dedicates the book to his daughter, Leonora. Without her, "the book would have been finished in half the time." This comical line is one that most parents understand. This man loved his daughter even though she distracted him from working. He loved her in spite of her actions. God gives that same kind of love to us. He loves us in spite of ourselves.

"But I say to you who listen: Love your enemies, do what is good to those who hate you, bless those who curse you, pray for those who mistreat you."

    Luke 6:27–28

———

Love is patient, love is kind. Love does not envy, is not boastful, is not arrogant, is not rude, is not self-seeking, is not irritable, and does not keep a record of wrongs.

    1 Corinthians 13:4–5

———

Above all, maintain constant love for one another, since love covers a multitude of sins.

    1 Peter 4:8

God's love was revealed among us in this way: God sent his one and only Son into the world so that we might live through him.

    1 John 4:9

———

And we have come to know and to believe the love that God has for us. God is love, and the one who remains in love remains in God, and God remains in him.

    1 John 4:16

Father, thank You for loving me. Thank You for showing the kind of love that no person ever could. I know that there are times that I am so unlovable; and yet, I know that You love me all the same. Father, allow me to take the love that You have for me and give it to others. Allow me to spread Your love to all of those that need it. Amen

Working on any kind of art takes a certain level of dedication. An artist has to recognize what their motives are. What do they want to accomplish with this piece? What kind of story do they want to tell with their song, their painting, or their writings? There is a message that has to be decided upon. They also have to live by their decisions. A mistake could be as dangerous as having to start over or leaving the project altogether. In life, are we living with the correct motivations, or are we pushing forward blindly—risking costly mistakes along the way?

But the LORD said to Samuel, "Do not look at his appearance or his stature because I have rejected him. Humans do not see what the LORD sees, for humans see what is visible, but the LORD sees the heart."

    1 Samuel 16:7

———

All a person's ways seem right to him, but the LORD weighs hearts.

    Proverbs 21:2

———

For am I now trying to persuade people, or God? Or am I striving to please people? If I were still trying to please people, I would not be a servant of Christ.

    Galatians 1:10

Do nothing out of selfish ambition or conceit, but in humility consider others as more important than yourselves.

Philippians 2:3

———

Instead, just as we have been approved by God to be entrusted with the gospel, so we speak, not to please people, but rather God, who examines our hearts.

1 Thessalonians 2:4

Lord, make my motives clear. Allow me to take the time to move forward with the correct motivations. Father, there are so many things that I need the correct motivations for. I have relationships, a job, a family, and my relationship with You, Lord. Allow me to work in all of these with the correct motivations. Allow me to live within these in a way that You would have me. Amen

One of the most difficult concepts in painting is something called layering. It is simple, but few artists can master the patience for it. It's described as painting from the bottom-up. You lay down your background color, then the next, then the next, and so on and so forth. It makes a brilliant picture of texture and color that is not found in just painting the object the same way someone would draw it. It's tedious but proves that the patience pays off. God calls us to be patient and it's obvious why . . . the best things in life take patience.

The end of a matter is better than its beginning; a patient spirit is better than a proud spirit.

Ecclesiastes 7:8

———

Now if we hope for what we do not see, we eagerly wait for it with patience.

Romans 8:25

———

My dear brothers and sisters, understand this: Everyone should be quick to listen, slow to speak, and slow to anger, for human anger does not accomplish God's righteousness.

James 1:19–20

Therefore, brothers and sisters, be patient until the Lord's coming. See how the farmer waits for the precious fruit of the earth and is patient with it until it receives the early and the late rains. You also must be patient. Strengthen your hearts, because the Lord's coming is near.

    James 5:7–8

———

The Lord does not delay his promise, as some understand delay, but is patient with you, not wanting any to perish but all to come to repentance.

    2 Peter 3:9

Heavenly Father, there are so many things that I want right now, and I know that's not right. I know that I have to be willing to wait. Father, I'm sorry that there are so many things in life that I have to be willing to wait for. Lord, put in me a spirit of patience so that I can wait for the things in life that You would have me wait for. Amen

It is something that some artists care about the most. They want to know that what they have done is good. They want to know that the hours of work they've put forth on something has gained approval. Non-Christians wonder why we praise God. I think it's rather simple. God gave something that is so overwhelmingly approved, that praise is just a natural by-product. The problem is that sometimes we forget just how good a gift His Son actually is.

I will praise God's name with song
and exalt him with thanksgiving.
    Psalm 69:30

———

Hallelujah!
Praise God in his sanctuary.
Praise him in his mighty expanse.
Praise him for his powerful acts;
praise him for his abundant greatness.
    Psalm 150:1–2

For from him and through him and to him are all things. To him be the glory forever. Amen

　　Romans 11:36

————

Now to him who is able to protect you from stumbling and to make you stand in the presence of his glory, without blemish and with great joy, to the only God our Savior, through Jesus Christ our Lord, be glory, majesty, power, and authority before all time, now and forever. Amen

　　Jude 24–25

*Father, thank You . . . You gave the ultimate gift.
You gave the gift that no person on this planet
could ever give. Your love for me is the reason
I praise You. It is Your overwhelming love that
makes it so easy to praise You. Sometimes I forget
that love, God, and for that I'm sorry . . . remind
me every day of just how good that love is. Amen*

PRIDE

There's a great deal of pride found in art. Many artists, musicians, and authors often compare their works to their children. It's natural for this to happen. You put hours, days, months, and sometimes years into something, and it becomes a part of who you are. Because of this, there is a lot of ego in the art world. It often shows up in times of critique, which is supposed to be used to make the work better. We so often look at our lives and think that it's the best that we've got to offer. We hate to receive criticism, but we should listen. If we can lay down our pride, we may hear something that makes our lives better.

When arrogance comes, disgrace follows,
but with humility comes wisdom.
    Proverbs 11:2

———

Everyone with a proud heart is detestable to the LORD;
be assured, he will not go unpunished.
    Proverbs 16:5

———

A person's pride will humble him,
but a humble spirit will gain honor.
    Proverbs 29:23

*Live in harmony with one another. Do not be proud;
instead, associate with the humble. Do not be wise
in your own estimation.*

 Romans 12:16

―――――

*For if anyone considers himself to be something
when he is nothing, he deceives himself.*

 Galatians 6:3

Lord, there are so many times that I cannot lay down my pride. I know that it is because I care too much about the things that maybe mean too little. Lord, soften my hard heart so that I may hear from those that wish to share wisdom with me. Allow me to be able to listen and actually take in what they have to say. Thank You, Father, for loving me when I am proud. Amen

Choir directors love a voice that can maintain a pure note that will often leave an audience awestruck. So many singers these days have a sound that is tainted by the singer's personal style, but a singer that is dedicated to the pureness of a note will simply sing the note with perfect vibration, perfect use of air, and perfect projection of voice. Purity is something that we should strive for in our daily lives. Though we cannot live perfectly, the attempt is something to be respected.

*God, create a clean heart for me
and renew a steadfast spirit within me.*

   Psalm 51:10

———

*"Blessed are the pure in heart, for they will see
God."*

   Matthew 5:8

———

*But put on the Lord Jesus Christ, and don't make
plans to gratify the desires of the flesh.*

   Romans 13:14

Flee sexual immorality! Every other sin a person commits is outside the body, but the person who is sexually immoral sins against his own body.

   1 Corinthians 6:18

———

If we confess our sins, he is faithful and righteous to forgive us our sins and to cleanse us from all unrighteousness.

   1 John 1:9

Heavenly Father, I know that there are parts in my life that have not shown purity. I know that I have fallen to temptation time and again, and I know that this is keeping me from living out a pure life. I know that we all fall, Lord, but allow me to seek after you so that I may fall less. Lord, thank You for constantly picking me up, no matter how many times I may fall. Amen

M. C. Escher is one of the most well-known artists to come out of the modern art era. His attention to detail is what he's known for in his work. Each of his works has individual lines that have a specific purpose. Chaos is not a word that would be used to describe any of his works. Everything is calculated. It is the result of self-control. People often tie self-control to the notion of not doing something, but self-control is also shown in the way that we do things. Consult Scripture and live with self-control; there is no telling what may come from it.

A person who does not control his temper
is like a city whose wall is broken down.
    Proverbs 25:28

No temptation has come upon you except what is
common to humanity. But God is faithful; he will
not allow you to be tempted beyond what you are
able, but with the temptation he will also provide a
way out so that you may be able to bear it.
    1 Corinthians 10:13

Finally brothers and sisters, whatever is true, whatever is honorable, whatever is just, whatever is pure, whatever is lovely, whatever is commendable—if there is any moral excellence and if there is anything praiseworthy—dwell on these things.

Philippians 4:8

———

Be sober-minded, be alert. Your adversary the devil is prowling around like a roaring lion, looking for anyone he can devour.

1 Peter 5:8

Lord Jesus, I have not lived a life that shows self-control. I have not carried myself in a way that shows I have self-control. Lord, allow me to walk in such a way that shows I can stand up to temptation. Be with me, Lord, so that I will not fall as easily. Allow me to keep my eyes on you, Lord. Amen

Most writers, musicians, and artists work knowing that there is a risk of never achieving success. There's a reason we have the phrase "starving artist." Monetary success is not always a guarantee that's tied to the work that we accomplish. So why risk it? Artists find success in accomplishment. Some may never have their book published, but they consider it a success that they wrote it in the first place. Some will never see their painting hanging in the Louvre, but it's a success to have it hanging in their home. Success doesn't always equal what we think it should. Dive into the Scriptures to see that success is success even if it is not exactly what you expected it to be.

*Take delight in the L*ORD,
and he will give you your heart's desires.
  Psalm 37:4

———

*Commit your activities to the L*ORD,
and your plans will be established.
  Proverbs 16:3

"For what will it benefit someone if he gains the whole world yet loses his life? Or what will anyone give in exchange for his life? For the Son of Man is going to come with his angels in the glory of his Father, and then he will reward each according to what he has done."

    Matthew 16:26–27

———

Humble yourselves before the Lord, and he will exalt you.

    James 4:10

Heavenly Father, thank You for the success in my life. Allow me to look at the moments of achievement that didn't go exactly as I think they should have as still a success. Father, allow me to look at the little moments through the same lens that I see the big moments. Allow me to have a spirit of humility so that I can see every success as a gift from You. Amen

There's a famous painting that most of us have probably seen. It's an oil painting of a man praying at a table. His bread is before him, soup waiting to be eaten, and his glasses lay on a large Bible. There's a sense of ritual to the painting. This man probably has done this every day for many years. There is no real sense of happiness or sadness, but reverence. The man looks as if he's literally thanking God for his "daily bread." How many of us can say that we hold the same level of thankfulness for the things God provides daily?

Give thanks to the LORD, for he is good;
his faithful love endures forever.
   Psalm 118:1

———

For we know that the one who raised the Lord Jesus
will also raise us with Jesus and present us with
you. Indeed, everything is for your benefit so that, as
grace extends through more and more people, it may
cause thanksgiving to increase to the glory of God.
   2 Corinthians 4:14–16

*Let the word of Christ dwell richly among you, in
all wisdom teaching and admonishing one another
through psalms, hymns, and spiritual songs,
singing to God with gratitude in your hearts.*

Colossians 3:16

———

*Rejoice always, pray constantly, give thanks in
everything; for this is God's will for you in Christ
Jesus.*

1 Thessalonians 5:16–18

———

*Every good and perfect gift is from above, coming
down from the Father of lights, who does not
change like shifting shadows.*

James 1:17

Lord, Thank you. I know that there are so many things that You do for me daily. I know that sometimes those things go overlooked. Father, thank You for the shelter over my head, the food that sustains me, and the relationships that make me a better person. Father, thank You for the big things as they come, but thank You for keeping the little things coming. Amen

Patronage has always been part of the arts. There's a little bit of risk in patronage. It is not that you are necessarily gambling on an artist so much as you are putting your trust in them. Many publishers, for instance, will provide book deals worth thousands of dollars in hopes that they will make that money back in selling those books. Why? Because they trust the artist; they trust that the author will provide on his or her part. Sometimes, though, the work will flop and money will be lost. It's amazing how we'll place our trust in people that can let us down but are so reluctant to trust in God.

The person who trusts in the LORD, *whose confidence indeed is the* LORD, *is blessed. He will be like a tree planted by water: it sends its roots out toward a stream, it doesn't fear when heat comes, and its foliage remains green. It will not worry in a year of drought or cease producing fruit.*

    Jeremiah 17:7–8

———

Wait for the LORD;
be strong, and let your heart be courageous.
Wait for the LORD.

    Psalm 27:14

I will be with you when you pass through the waters, and when you pass through the rivers, they will not overwhelm you. You will not be scorched when you walk through the fire, and the flame will not burn you.

Isaiah 43:2

———

And my God will supply all your needs according to his riches in glory in Christ Jesus.

Philippians 4:19

———

This is the confidence we have before him: If we ask anything according to his will, he hears us.

1 John 5:14

Father, I know that I can trust You and that You will not let me down. I'm sorry that my actions have not shown that. I'm sorry that I have not been obedient, Lord. Allow me to trust in You again. Soften my heart so that the relationship I've damaged can be mended again. Amen

One of the most important things that a songwriter can have is wisdom. Songs get lost in time, but every now and again, we come across lines that hold such wisdom that they almost get applied to everyday life even though some musicians don't exactly live the wisest of lives. So, how does this wisdom sneak into their songs? A great deal of these musicians will tell you that it was wisdom shared by someone they held deep admiration for. Scripture tells us the importance of seeking out wisdom in hopes that this wisdom will become a part of our lives.

Teach us to number our days carefully
so that we may develop wisdom in our hearts.
    Psalm 90:12

———

Do not be conformed to this age, but be transformed
by the renewing of your mind, so that you may
discern what is the good, pleasing, and perfect will
of God.
    Romans 12:2

Yet to those who are called, both Jews and Greeks, Christ is the power of God and the wisdom of God, because God's foolishness is wiser than human wisdom, and God's weakness is stronger than human strength.

1 Corinthians 1:24–25

———

Now if any of you lacks wisdom, he should ask God—who gives to all generously and ungrudgingly—and it will be given to him.

James 1:5

Lord, thank You for placing wise people in my life. I know that I do not always listen, but still, You have continued to place these people in my life. Father, put in me a heart that desires to listen to the wisdom others might have for me. Allow me to take that wisdom and apply it, Lord, so that I may serve You better. Amen